Poorman Doodles
Coloring Fun for Grown Ups

30 Exciting Drawings By Master Doodle Artist Kevin Poorman

Book designed and published by Puzzle Cuts   www.puzzlecuts.com

About the Artist

Kevin Poorman is an artist, photographer and puzzle-maker living in Lorton, Virginia. He grew up in Southern Indiana where his family owned and operated an artist supplies and picture framing business catering to area artists and art students attending Vincennes University.

Kevin's preferred art medium is pen and black ink. This book contains 30 of Kevin's pen and ink doodle art drawings, offering hours of relaxing enjoyment coloring the varied intricate patterns and designs.

In the last few years, Kevin ventured into making jigsaw puzzles from his artwork and photographs. His puzzles are available at several historical venues in Northern Virginia, including George Mason's plantation at Gunston Hall, the Manassas National Battlefield, the Fairfax City Museum, as well as various gift and specialty shops, including Puzzle Palooza, Etc., in Occoquan, and T & K Treasures Specialty Gifts in Clifton, Virginia.

Please see the full line of Kevin's drawings, photographs and puzzles at www.puzzlecuts.com .

Email comments to: puzzlecuts@gmail.com

Enjoy coloring!

This blank page serves as a
blotter page to absorb any
marker ink that might bleed
through while coloring.

K.Poorman '15

This blank page serves as a blotter page to absorb any marker ink that might bleed through while coloring.

This blank page serves as a
blotter page to absorb any
marker ink that might bleed
through while coloring.

See Kevin's other books on
Amazon.com.

Search "Poorman Doodles"

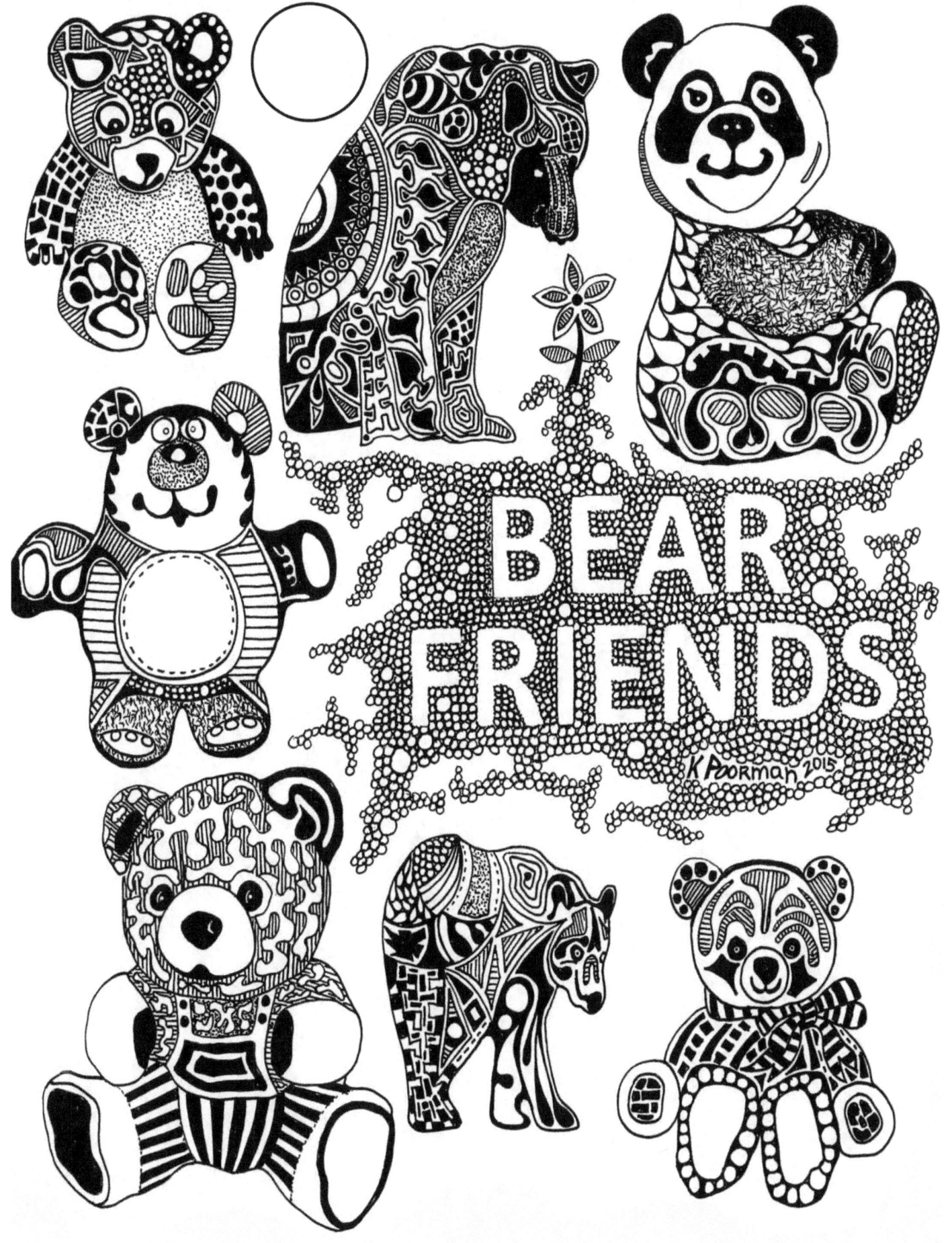

This blank page serves as a blotter page to absorb any marker ink that might bleed through while coloring.

This blank page serves as a
blotter page to absorb any
marker ink that might bleed
through while coloring.

See Kevin's other books on
Amazon.com.

Search "Poorman Doodles"

Kevin Poorman 2010

This blank page serves as a
blotter page to absorb any
marker ink that might bleed
through while coloring.

This blank page serves as a
blotter page to absorb any
marker ink that might bleed
through while coloring.

This blank page serves as a blotter page to absorb any marker ink that might bleed through while coloring.

This blank page serves as a blotter page to absorb any marker ink that might bleed through while coloring.

This blank page serves as a
blotter page to absorb any
marker ink that might bleed
through while coloring.

This blank page serves as a blotter page to absorb any marker ink that might bleed through while coloring.

K.Poorman '15

This blank page serves as a blotter page to absorb any marker ink that might bleed through while coloring.

This blank page serves as a blotter page to absorb any marker ink that might bleed through while coloring.

This blank page serves as a
blotter page to absorb any
marker ink that might bleed
through while coloring.

This blank page serves as a blotter page to absorb any marker ink that might bleed through while coloring.

K. Poorman '15

This blank page serves as a
blotter page to absorb any
marker ink that might bleed
through while coloring.

This blank page serves as a
blotter page to absorb any
marker ink that might bleed
through while coloring.

This blank page serves as a
blotter page to absorb any
marker ink that might bleed
through while coloring.

This blank page serves as a
blotter page to absorb any
marker ink that might bleed
through while coloring.

See Kevin's other books on
Amazon.com.

Search "Poorman Doodles"

Entangled

This blank page serves as a blotter page to absorb any marker ink that might bleed through while coloring.

Entangled Too

This blank page serves as a
blotter page to absorb any
marker ink that might bleed
through while coloring.

See Kevin's other books on
Amazon.com.

Search "Poorman Doodles"

The Owl

This blank page serves as a
blotter page to absorb any
marker ink that might bleed
through while coloring.

See Kevin's other books on
Amazon.com.

Search "Poorman Doodles"

This blank page serves as a blotter page to absorb any marker ink that might bleed through while coloring.

This blank page serves as a blotter page to absorb any marker ink that might bleed through while coloring.

This blank page serves as a
blotter page to absorb any
marker ink that might bleed
through while coloring.

K. Poorman

This blank page serves as a
blotter page to absorb any
marker ink that might bleed
through while coloring.

This blank page serves as a blotter page to absorb any marker ink that might bleed through while coloring.

This blank page serves as a
blotter page to absorb any
marker ink that might bleed
through while coloring.

This blank page serves as a blotter page to absorb any marker ink that might bleed through while coloring.

This blank page serves as a blotter page to absorb any marker ink that might bleed through while coloring.